Collins

Maths Frameworking

Intervention Workbook

Chris Pearce

William Collins's dream of knowledge for all began with the publication of his first book in 1819. A self-educated mill worker, he not only enriched millions of lives, but also founded a flourishing publishing house. Today, staying true to this spirit, Collins books are packed with inspiration, innovation and practical expertise. They place you at the centre of a world of possibility and give you exactly what you need to explore it.

Collins. Freedom to teach.

Published by Collins
An imprint of HarperCollins*Publishers*
77–85 Fulham Palace Road
Hammersmith
London
W6 8JB

Browse the complete Collins catalogue at
www.harpercollins.co.uk

Acknowledgements
The publishers wish to thank the following for permission to reproduce photographs. Every effort has been made to trace copyright holders and to obtain their permission for the use of copyright materials. The publishers will gladly receive any information enabling them to rectify any error or omission at the first opportunity.

Cover Image: Carl Schneider/Getty Images

All other images © HarperCollins*Publishers*

British Library Cataloguing in Publication Data
A Catalogue record for this publication is available from the British Library.

Commissioned by Katie Sergeant
Project managed by Elektra Media Ltd
Copy-edited and proofread by Philippa Boxer
Illustrations by Ann Paganuzzi
Typeset by Jouve India Private Limited
Cover design by Angela English

Printed and bound by Martins the Printers

How to use this book

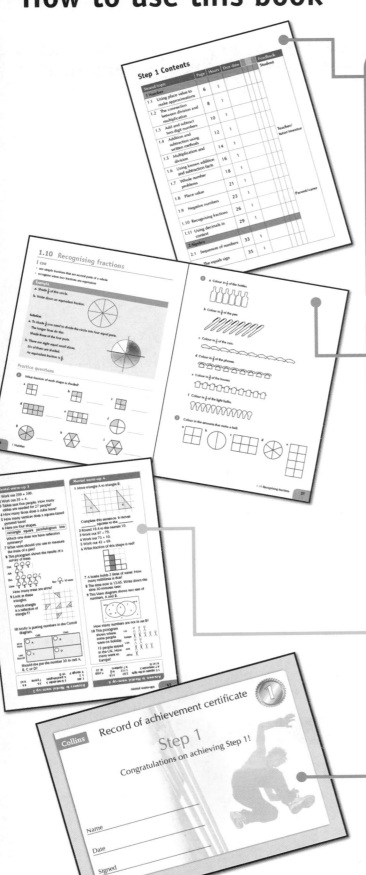

Organise your learning

The Contents table at the start of the Workbook shows the topics you are going to cover.

- Your teacher or tutor can set a date for you to complete each topic by.
- You can give a traffic light colour for each topic to show how you feel it went.
- You, your teacher and your parent or carer can write comments.

Work through each topic step by step

For each topic, there are:

- Clear learning objectives
- Worked examples to show you how to answer the questions
- Practice questions to help you consolidate what you have learnt. A glossary and answers are available on the Collins website.

At the end of each chapter, there's a comments box for your teacher or tutor to fill in on how you did.

Practise your mental maths

Try the mental maths questions at the end of the Workbook to see what you have learned.

Celebrate your progress

When you finish the Workbook, your teacher or tutor can fill in the Record of achievement certificate for you to keep.

Step 1 Contents

1 Number

1.1 Using place value to make approximations

I can

- round any positive integer less than 1000 to the nearest 10 or 100
- round some four-digit numbers to the nearest 1000

Example

The price of a second-hand car is £785. Round this number to the nearest 100.

Solution

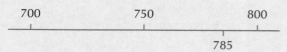

785 is between 700 and 800.

750 is halfway between 700 and 800.

785 is larger than 750.

7 is the hundreds digit in 785.

It is closer to 800 than it is to 700.

785 is 800 to the nearest 100.

Practice questions

1   Round each of these numbers to the nearest 10.

a 64 _____   b 72 _____   c 89 _____

d 23 _____   e 65 _____   f 14 _____

g 26 _____   h 31 _____   i 25 _____

j 77 _____   k 66 _____   l 34 _____

2 Round each of these numbers to the nearest 100.

a 734 _____

b 576 _____

c 212 _____

d 788 _____

e 899 _____

f 150 _____

g 129 _____

h 233 _____

i 643 _____

j 349 _____

k 743 _____

l 379 _____

3 Round each of these numbers to the nearest 1000.

a 3400 _____

b 1200 _____

c 7800 _____

d 8900 _____

e 6100 _____

f 6500 _____

g 9200 _____

h 5500 _____

i 6800 _____

j 3200 _____

k 4500 _____

l 1300 _____

4 Round the prices in this table to the nearest £10 and £100. The first one has been done for you.

Price	To the nearest £10	To the nearest £100
£339	£340	£300
£182		
£715		
£528		
£891		
£219		
£665		

1.2 The connection between division and multiplication

I can

• use multiplication facts to write down associated division facts

Example

Here is a multiplication fact: **12 × 9 = 108**

Use this to write down two division facts.

Solution

One fact is $108 \div 9 = 12$ *because twelve 9s make 108.*

Another fact is $108 \div 12 = 9$ *because nine 12s make 108.*

If you are given a multiplication fact you can always write down two division facts.

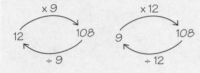

Practice questions

1 Here is a multiplication fact: $7 \times 8 = 56$

Write down these answers. $56 \div 7 =$ _____ $56 \div 8 =$ _____

2 Here is a multiplication fact: $6 \times 12 = 72$

Write down these answers. $72 \div 6 =$ _____ $72 \div 12 =$ _____

3 Look at this multiplication: $15 \times 5 = 75$

Use this to write down two divisions. _____ and _____.

4 Here are some multiplication facts:

$9 \times 7 = 63$ $\qquad$ $12 \times 7 = 84$ $\qquad$ $13 \times 4 = 52$ $\qquad$ $16 \times 5 = 80$

Use them to complete these divisions.

$84 \div 12 =$ _____ $\qquad$ $52 \div 4 =$ _____ $\qquad$ $80 \div 5 =$ _____ $\qquad$ $63 \div 9 =$ _____

5 Here are some multiplication facts:

$2 \times 50 = 100$ $\qquad$ $4 \times 25 = 100$ $\qquad$ $5 \times 20 = 100$ $\qquad$ $10 \times 10 = 100$

Use them to complete these divisions.

$100 \div 2 =$ _____ $\qquad$ $100 \div 5 \ \ =$ _____ $\qquad$ $100 \div 10 =$ _____

$100 \div 4 =$ _____ $\qquad$ $100 \div 50 =$ _____ $\qquad$ $100 \div 20 =$ _____

1.3 Add and subtract two-digit numbers

I can

* add and subtract two-digit numbers in my head

Example

a Add together this pair of numbers. 52 + 29

b Subtract this pair of numbers.   52 – 29

Solution

a 50 + 20 = 70   Add the tens of each number.

  2 + 9 = 11   Add the units of each number.

  70 + 11 = 81   Then add the two separate answers.

b You can draw or imagine a line if you wish.

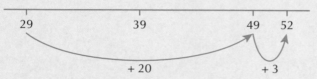

Count on from 29 to 52.

From 29 to 49 is 20.

From 49 to 52 is 3.

52 – 29 = 20 + 3 = 23

You may know different methods. Use those if you prefer them.

Practice questions

1 Add together each pair of numbers.

  a 47 + 21 = _____   **b** 57 + 35 = _____   **c** 62 + 32 = _____

d 76 + 54 = _____   **e** 47 + 34 = _____   **f** 56 + 32 = _____

g 72 + 41 = _____   **h** 88 + 33 = _____   **i** 96 + 21 = _____

2 Work out these subtractions.

a 47 − 21 = _____   **b** 57 − 35 = _____   **c** 62 − 32 = _____

d 76 − 54 = _____   **e** 47 − 34 = _____   **f** 56 − 32 = _____

g 72 − 41 = _____   **h** 88 − 33 = _____   **i** 96 − 21 = _____

3 Use any method to work out these additions and subtractions.

a 70 + 34 = _____   **b** 70 − 34 = _____   **c** 66 + 23 = _____

d 66 − 23 = _____   **e** 46 + 39 = _____   **f** 46 − 39 = _____

g 67 + 21 = _____   **h** 67 − 21 = _____

1.4 Addition and subtraction using written methods

I can

- add and subtract three-digit numbers using written methods

a Work out this addition. $654 + 183$

b Work out this subtraction. $654 - 183$

Solution

Write the numbers in columns.

a
```
  6 5 4
+ 1 8 3
  8 3 7
    1
```

First add the units: $4 + 3 = 7$.

Then add the tens: $5 + 8 = 13$; write down 3, carry 1.

Now add the hundreds: $6 + 1 + 1$ carried $= 8$.

The answer is 837.

b
```
  5 6 1 5 4
-   1 8 3
    4 7 1
```

First subtract the units: $4 - 3 = 1$.

Then subtract the tens: 5 is smaller than 8, so borrow from the hundreds and do $15 - 8 = 7$.

Now subtract the hundreds: $5 - 1 = 4$

The answer is 471.

Practice questions

 1 Use a written method to work out these additions. Show your working.

    a 174 + 75 = _____   **b** 345 + 128 = _____   **c** 173 + 566 = _____

    d 286 + 45 = _____   **e** 365 + 209 = _____   **f** 376 + 545 = _____

    g 75 + 333 = _____   **h** 208 + 334 = _____   **i** 265 + 716 = _____

2 Use a written method to work out these subtractions. Show your working.

    a 286 – 142 = _____   **b** 765 – 234 = _____   **c** 718 – 34 = _____

    d 174 – 57 = _____   **e** 362 – 149 = _____   **f** 634 – 509 = _____

    g 977 – 326 = _____   **h** 423 – 66 = _____   **i** 265 – 119 = _____

1.5 Multiplication and division

I can

- multiply and divide two-digit numbers by 2, 3, 4 or 5
- divide two-digit numbers by 2, 3 4 or 5, including remainders

Example

a Work out this multiplication.　　78 x 3

b Work out this division.　　　　78 ÷ 3

Solution

Write out the calculations neatly.

a
$$
\begin{array}{r}
7\,8 \\
\times\ \ 3 \\
\hline
2\,3\,4 \\
{\scriptstyle 2}
\end{array}
$$

First 8 × 3 = 24; write down 4, carry 2.

Then 7 × 3 = 21; 21 + 2 carried = 23.

The answer is 234.

b
$$
\begin{array}{r}
2\,6 \\
3\overline{)7\,{}^{1}8}
\end{array}
$$

First 7 ÷ 3 = 2 remainder 1.

Then 18 ÷ 3 = 6.

The answer is 26.

You should know the multiplication tables for 2, 3, 4, and 5.

Practice questions

　Work out these multiplications. Show your working.

　　a 37 x 2 = _____　　　　**b** 19 x 5 = _____　　　　**c** 23 x 3 = _____

d 62 x 3 = _____   **e** 74 x 4 = _____   **f** 55 x 5 = _____

g 58 x 4 = _____   **h** 32 x 8 = _____   **i** 54 x 8 = _____

2 Work out these divisions. Show your working.

a 48 ÷ 2 = _____   **b** 46 ÷ 3 = _____   **c** 60 ÷ 4 = _____

d 63 ÷ 5 = _____   **e** 54 ÷ 3 = _____   **f** 62 ÷ 5 = _____

g 95 ÷ 4 = _____   **h** 75 ÷ 5 = _____   **i** 87 ÷ 2 = _____

1.6 Using known addition and subtraction facts

I can
- recall addition and subtraction facts up to 20
- use known facts to solve problems involving larger numbers

Example

Work out the following additions and subtraction.

a $65 + 7$ **b** $88 - 30$ **c** $63 + 26$

Solution

Look for easy methods, like these:

a 65 is $60 + 5$ $60 + 5 + 7 = 60 + 12 = 72$

b $8 - 3 = 5$ so $80 - 30 = 50$ and $88 - 30 = 50 + 8 = 58$

c $63 + 26 = 60 + 3 + 20 + 6 = 60 + 20 + 3 + 6 = 80 + 9 = 89$

You can probably do these in your head. There is no need to write them out.

Practice questions

1 Work out these additions.

a $7 + 12 =$ _____ **b** $13 + 14 =$ _____ **c** $13 + 6 =$ _____

d $44 + 30 =$ _____ **e** $50 + 35 =$ _____ **f** $65 + 4 =$ _____

g $216 + 13 =$ _____ **h** $350 + 14 =$ _____ **i** $257 + 13 =$ _____

2 Work out these subtractions.

a $19 - 7 =$ _____ **b** $18 - 6 =$ _____ **c** $17 - 13 =$ _____

d $90 - 30 =$ _____ **e** $73 - 30 =$ _____ **f** $82 - 50 =$ _____

g $92 - 40 =$ _____ **h** $106 - 30 =$ _____ **i** $114 - 40 =$ _____

3 Add together these numbers.

    a 15 and 16 _____   **b** 25 and 16 _____   **c** 7 and 13   _____

    d 17 and 13 _____   **e** 7, 8 and 9 _____   **f** 7, 18 and 19 _____

4 Fill in the missing number in these calculations.

    a _____ + 7 = 18   **b** 24 – _____ = 15   **c** 13 + _____ = 37

    d _____ – 18 = 9   **e** 23 – _____ = 9   **f** 14 + _____ = 59

5 Look at the numbers in the box, then answer the questions.

40	50	60	70	90	120	140	160

    a Write down two numbers that add to make 100. _____ and _____

    b Write down two numbers with a sum of 200. _____ and _____

    c Write down two numbers with a difference of 40. _____ and _____

    d Write down two numbers with a difference of 90. _____ and _____

1.7 Whole number problems

I can

- decide which operation to use to solve a problem
- solve division problems with remainders

Example

There are 32 people waiting to travel in a taxi.

Each taxi can take five passengers.

How many taxis do they need?

Solution

This is a division question because you have to divide the group of people up between the taxis.

$32 \div 5 = 6$ remainder 2

They can fill six taxis but there are still two people left over.

They need seven taxis.

Practice questions

1 Work out these divisions. They all have remainders.

a $29 \div 4 = $ _____ remainder _____   b $31 \div 5 = $ _____ remainder _____

c $15 \div 2 = $ _____ remainder _____   d $20 \div 3 = $ _____ remainder _____

2 There are 23 biscuits in a packet. Four people share them equally.

How many does each person have? _____ biscuits

3 There are five cereal bars in a box. Jasmine buys eight boxes.

How many cereal bars does Jasmine buy? _____ bars

4 There are 45 guests at a meal. They are sitting at tables. Each table can seat six people.

How many tables are needed? _____ tables

5 Ali, Rob and Carol are looking at how much money they have. Ali has £32, Rob has £14 and Carol has £57.

a How much do they have all together?   _____

b How much more than Rob does Carol have?   _____

c Carol has six two-pound coins and the rest is in five-pound notes.

Work out how many five-pound notes she has. _____

d Carol and Rob put their money together and share it out equally between the two of them.

How much does each one get?   _____

6 Mintees are sweets that come in packets of 36

a Work out the number of Mintees in five packets.   _____ Mintees

b If five people share one packet equally, how many Mintees will each person get?

_____ Mintees

c Merry has a packet of Mintees. He eats 14 and gives five away. How many are left?

_____ Mintees

7 A bus has 52 seats and 23 passengers. At a bus stop four people get off and 12 get on.

How many empty seats are there on the bus?   _____ empty seats

8 There are eight seats in a large taxi.

How many taxis are needed to carry 50 people?   _____ taxis

1.8 Place value

I can

• understand place value in numbers up to thousands

Example

Here is a number: 1062

a Write the number in words.

b Write down the tens digit.

Solution

a The number is one thousand and sixty-two.

b The tens digit is 6.   *The 1 is the thousands digit, the 0 is the hundreds digit and the 2 is the units digit.*

Practice questions

1   Write these numbers in figures.

    a twenty-seven   _____

    b thirty-four   _____

    c one hundred and fifty-two   _____

    d three hundred and eight   _____

    e seven hundred and forty   _____

    f one thousand two hundred and three   _____

27

twenty-seven

2   Write these numbers in words.

    a 35   _____

    b 179   _____

    c 204   _____

    d 990   _____

    e 1678   _____

3 Write down

   a the tens digit in 3412. _____

   b the hundreds digit in 3052. _____

   c the units digit in three hundred and sixty-seven. _____

4 Write the price of each car on its windscreen in numbers.

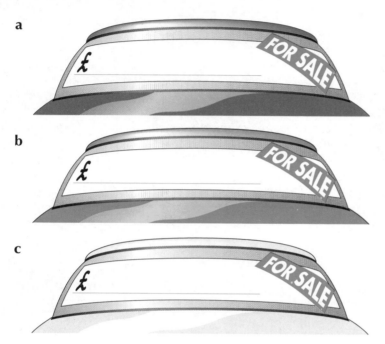

   a two thousand five hundred pounds

   b one thousand one hundred and ninety-nine pounds

   c two thousand and ninety-nine pounds

5 Which is the cheapest car in Question 4?

_____

1.9 Negative numbers

I can

- order a set of positive and negative numbers
- calculate a temperature rise and fall across 0 °C

Example

Here are some temperatures in degrees C: **2, –3, 4, 5, –6**

Put them in order, from lowest to highest.

Solution

You can draw a number line to help you, and mark the numbers on it.

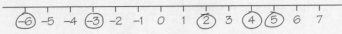

The lowest are on the left, the highest are on the right.

In order they are –6, –3, 2, 4, 5.

Practice questions

1   Here are some sets of temperatures in degrees C.

Put each set of temperatures in order, from lowest to highest.

a   2, 7, –2, 3, –3, 0   _____

b   –7, 4, –5, 6, 2   _____

c   9, 6, –5, 4, –3, 0   _____

d   6, 4, –2, –3, 9, –1   _____

2   Look at the thermometers and answer the questions.

a

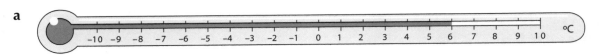

If the temperature increases by 3 °C what will the temperature be? _____°C

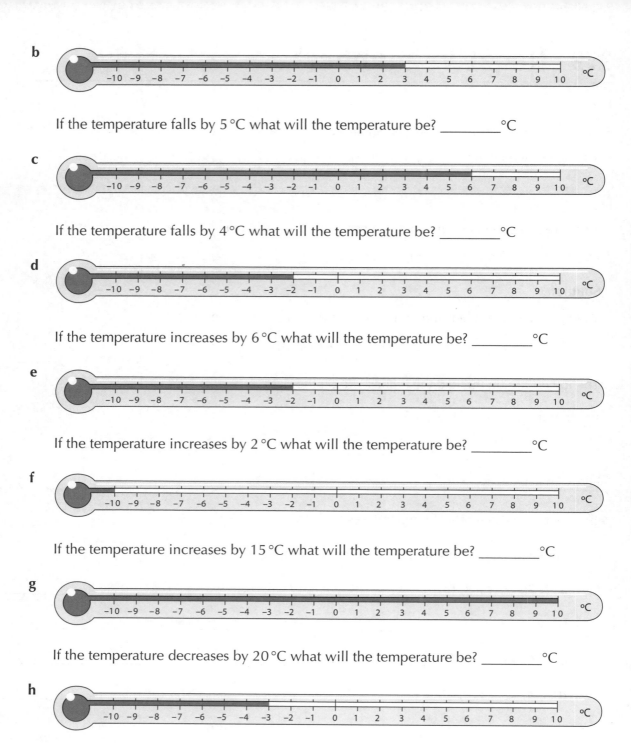

b

If the temperature falls by 5 °C what will the temperature be? _____°C

c

If the temperature falls by 4 °C what will the temperature be? _____°C

d

If the temperature increases by 6 °C what will the temperature be? _____°C

e

If the temperature increases by 2 °C what will the temperature be? _____°C

f

If the temperature increases by 15 °C what will the temperature be? _____°C

g

If the temperature decreases by 20 °C what will the temperature be? _____°C

h

If the temperature increases by 12 °C what will the temperature be? _____°C

3 Write down the temperatures shown on the thermometer.

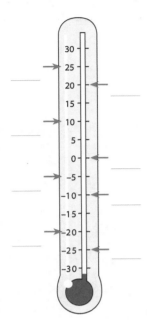

4 Fill in the missing numbers on the number lines.

a

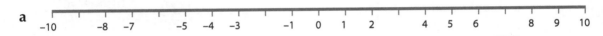

-10   -8   -7   -5   -4   -3   -1   0   1   2   4   5   6   8   9   10

b

-9   -7   -5   -3   -2   1   2   3   4   5   8   9   10

c

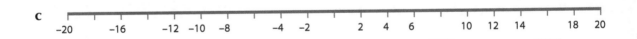

-20   -16   -12   -10   -8   -4   -2   2   4   6   10   12   14   18   20

d

-100   -80   -70   -40   -30   -20   0   10   20   30   50   60   80   90   100

1.10 Recognising fractions

I can

- use simple fractions that are several parts of a whole
- recognise when two fractions are equivalent

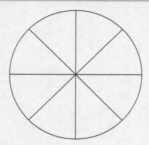
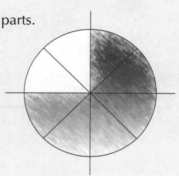
Practice questions

1 What fraction of each shape is shaded?

a _____

b _____

c _____

d 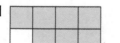 _____

e 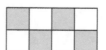 _____

f _____

g _____

h _____

i _____

2 **a** Colour in $\frac{1}{3}$ of the bottles.

b Colour in $\frac{3}{4}$ of the pen

c Colour in $\frac{1}{5}$ of the cars.

d Colour in $\frac{2}{3}$ of the phones.

e Colour in $\frac{3}{5}$ of the houses.

f Colour in $\frac{1}{4}$ of the light bulbs.

3 Colour in the amounts that make a half.

a 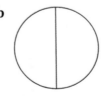 **b** 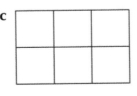 **c** 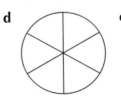 **d** **e**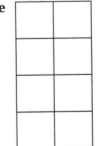

4   Colour in the amounts that make a quarter.

a 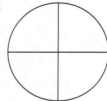   b 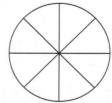   c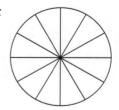

5   Colour in the equivalent fractions for a third.

a    b 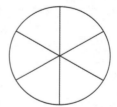   c

6   Colour in the equivalent fractions for a fifth.

a 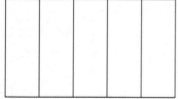   b

c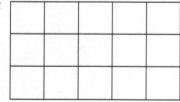

1.11 Using decimals in context

I can

- use decimals and understand place value in decimals in a context, such as money

Example

a Write 1620 pence in pounds.

b Write 124 millimetres in centimetres.

Solution

a There are 100 pence in one pound.

1620 pence = 16 pounds and 20 pence = £16.20.

b There are 10 millimetres in one centimetre.

124 millimetres = 12 centimetres and 4 millimetres = 12.4 centimetres.

Practice questions

 a Write down the amount of money in each of the piles below. Give your answers in pounds.

_____ _____ _____ _____

b Put a circle around the largest amount. Put a square around the smallest amount.

2 Write these amounts of money in pounds.

a 250 pence = £ _____

b 408 pence = £ _____

c 1287 pence = £ _____

d 4000 pence = £ _____

3 Write these amounts in pence.

    a £7 = _____ pence   **b** £12.50 = _____ pence

    c £0.80 = _____ pence   **d** £0.05 = _____ pence

4 45 millimetres is equal to 4.5 centimetres.

Write these lengths in centimetres.

    a 23 mm = _____ cm   **b** 51 mm = _____ cm

    c 60 mm = _____ cm   **d** 8 mm = _____ cm

5 5.6 centimetres is equal to 56 millimetres.

Write these lengths in millimetres.

    a 6.2 cm = _____ mm   **b** 12.5 cm = _____ mm

    c 25 cm = _____ mm   **d** 0.2 cm = _____ mm

6 Write the tenths from 0 to 1 as decimals.

7 Fill in the missing numbers on the number lines. The first one has been done for you.

a
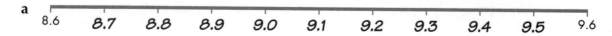

b

c

d

8 Write the hundredths from 0 to 0.1 as decimals.

9 Fill in the missing numbers on the number lines. The first one has been done for you.

a

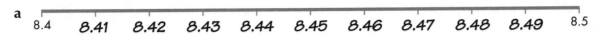

b

c

Comments, next steps, misconceptions

1 Number

2 Algebra

2.1 Sequences of numbers

I can

• recognise patterns in sequences of numbers

Example

Here is a sequence of numbers: 9   13   17   21   25

Work out the next two numbers.

Solution

The numbers increase by 4 each time.

The next number is 25 + 4 = 29.

The number after 29 is 29 + 4 = 33.

Practice questions

1   Write the next two numbers in each of these number sequences using the rule shown.

   a The rule is add on 2 each time.

     22   24   26   28   _____   _____

   b The rule is add on 5 each time.

     7   12   17   22   _____   _____

   c The rule is subtract 3 each time.

     30   27   24   21   _____   _____

   d The rule is subtract 10 each time.

     95   85   75   65   _____   _____

e The rule is double each time.

1   2   4   8   _____   _____

2   Write the next two numbers in each of these number sequences.

a 3   5   7   9   _____   _____

b 42   44   46   48   _____   _____

c 30   35   40   45   _____   _____

d 1   7   13   19   _____   _____

e 40   37   34   31   _____   _____

f 50   44   38   32   _____   _____

g 10   21   32   43   _____   _____

h 120   116   112   108   _____   _____

3   Write in the missing numbers in each of these number sequences.

a 12   16   _____   24   28   32   _____   40

b 17   22   27   _____   _____   42   47   52   _____   62

c 99   96   93   _____   87   _____   81   78   _____   72   69

d 46   42   _____   _____   _____   26   22   18   _____

2.2 The equals sign

I can

• use the equals sign (=) correctly

Example

Here are some numbers with gaps between them: 9 _____ 3 _____ 4 _____ 2

Put the signs +, − and = in the gaps to make a correct statement.

Solution

Try putting the signs in different places.

The correct way is: $9 - 3 = 4 + 2$.

$9 - 3$ and $4 + 2$ are both equal to 6.

Practice questions

1. Put the signs + and = in each of these to make a correct statement.

   a 9 _____ 3 _____ 6   **b** 12 _____ 2 _____ 14

   c 6 _____ 1 _____ 7   **d** 11 _____ 3 _____ 8

2. Put the signs − and = in each of these to make a correct statement.

   a 9 _____ 3 _____ 6   **b** 12 _____ 14 _____ 2

   c 6 _____ 7 _____ 1   **d** 11 _____ 3 _____ 8

3. Put the signs +, − and = in each of these to make a correct statement.

   a 12 ____ 3 ____ 18 ____ 3   **b** 3 ____ 8 ____ 5 ____ 6   **c** 10 ____ 6 ____ 8 ____ 4

4. Put the signs +, × and = in each of these to make a correct statement.

   a 3 ____ 5 ____ 2 ____ 4   **b** 3 ____ 5 ____ 8 ____ 7   **c** 6 ____ 3 ____ 3 ____ 3

5 Put signs in each of these to make correct statements.

a 24 = 4 _____ 6

b 24 _____ 4 = 6

c 19 = 12 _____ 7

d 19 _____ 12 = 7

6 Put signs in each of these to make correct statements.

a 12 = 3 _____ 4 _____ 5

b 4 _____ 3 = 2 _____ 6

c 5 _____ 4 = 8 _____ 7

d 2 _____ 5 = 6 _____ 4

e 5 _____ 1 = 12 _____ 2

f 50 _____ 8 = 25 _____ 17

Comments, next steps, misconceptions

2 Algebra

3 Geometry and measures

3.1 Classify 2D and 3D shapes

I can

- understand the properties of 2D shapes, including reflective symmetry
- understand the properties of 3D shapes

Example

a What is the name of this shape?

b Draw a line of symmetry on the shape.

Solution

a The shape has six sides, so it is a hexagon.

b There are two lines of symmetry.

Both are drawn here.

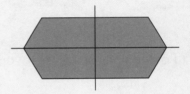

Remember: if you fold a shape on a line of symmetry, the two parts will match exactly.

Practice questions

1 Draw each of these shapes onto the dotty grid.

Rectangle   Isosceles triangle   Right-angled triangle

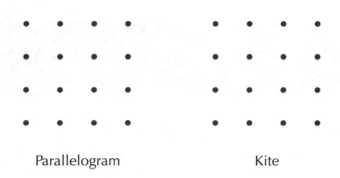

Parallelogram   Kite

2 Which shapes in Question 1 have a line of symmetry?

_____

3 Draw a line of symmetry onto each of the following diagrams.

4 Draw all of the lines of symmetry onto these letters.

5 Draw the lines of symmetry onto each of these road signs.

6 Choose the correct name for these 3D shapes from the list below. Write the name underneath each shape.

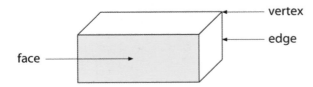

Pyramid　　　　**Cuboid**　　　　**Sphere**　　　　**Cube**　　　　**Tetrahedron**

a

_____

b

_____

c

_____

d

_____

7 A cuboid has six faces, eight vertices and twelve edges.

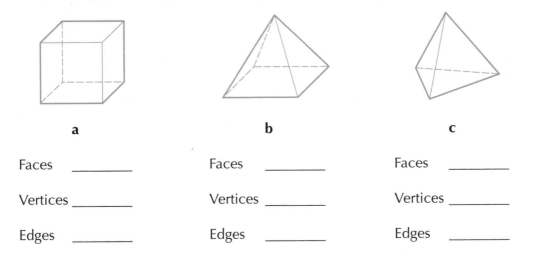

vertex

edge

face

How many faces, vertices and edges do these 3D shapes have?

a

b

c

Faces _____　　　Faces _____　　　Faces _____

Vertices _____　　Vertices _____　　Vertices _____

Edges _____　　　Edges _____　　　Edges _____

3.2 Nets of 3D shapes

I can

- recognise nets of 3D shapes, such as cubes, cuboids, triangular prisms and square-based pyramids
- understand the properties of 3D shapes

Example

Here is the net of a cube.

It is made into a cube.

a What face is opposite face A?

b What face is opposite face B?

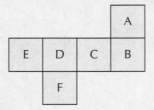

Solution

Try to imagine the shape made up. You can cut it out of paper if you wish.

a F is opposite face A.

b D is opposite face B.

Practice questions

1   Circle the net that will make an open box in the shape of a cube. The base has been shaded to help you.

a

b
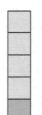

c

d
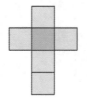

2   Add one more square to make the net of a cube.

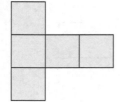

3 Add one more shape to make the net of a cuboid.

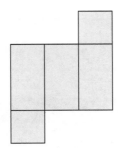

4 Add one more shape to make the net of a triangular prism.

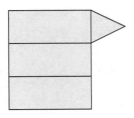

5 Here is a net.

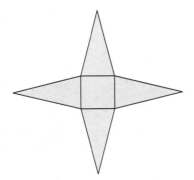

a What shape is it a net of? _____

b What type of triangles are they? _____

6 Circle the net that is **not** the net of a cube.

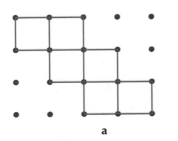 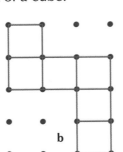 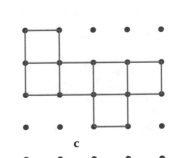

a   b   c

3.3 Working with 2D shapes

I can

- reflect shapes in a vertical or horizontal mirror line

Reflect this shape in both lines to give a shape with two lines of symmetry.

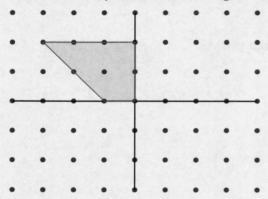

Solution

First reflect the shape in one line.

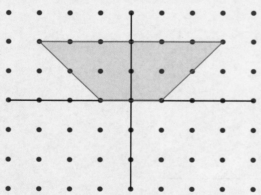

Then reflect both parts in the other line.

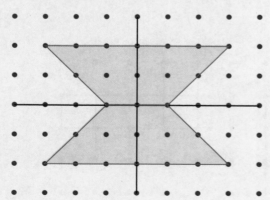

Practice questions

1 Complete these half-shapes by reflecting them in the mirror lines marked.

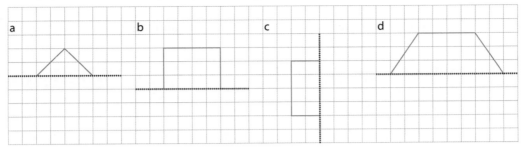

2 Reflect these shapes in the mirror lines shown.

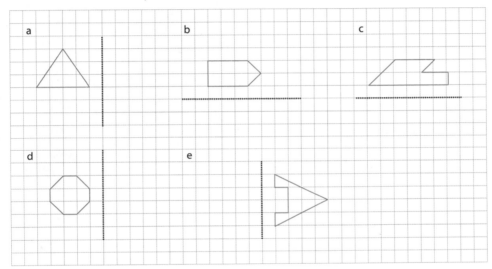

3 This pattern has two lines of symmetry.

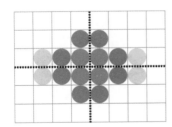

Complete each pattern below by reflecting it in both the horizontal and vertical axes of symmetry. Make sure each one has two lines of symmetry.

a

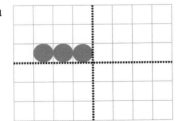

b

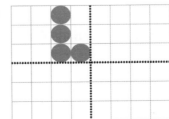

3.4 Position and movement

I can

- describe changes of position using words like 'up', 'down', 'left' and 'right'

Example

Describe how to move from shape A to shape B.

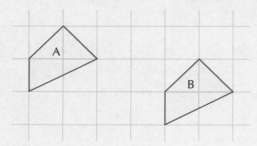

Solution

Choose the same corner in each shape and describe the move.

It is four squares to the right and one square down.

Practice questions

1 Complete these sentences. Write a number and 'up', 'down', 'left' or 'right'.

a To move from shape A to shape B move _____ squares _____

b To move from shape D to shape B move _____ squares _____

c To move from shape D to shape C move _____ squares _____

2 **a** Move the shape three squares to the right.

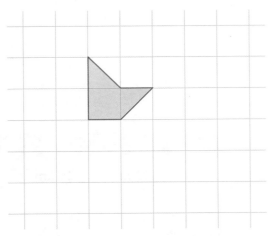

Label the new shape X.

b Move the shape down two squares.

Label the new shape Y.

c Describe the move from shape X to the first shape.

_____

d Describe the move from shape Y to the first shape.

_____

3 **a** Move this shape four squares to the right.

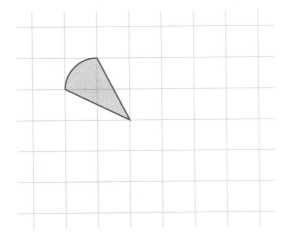

Label the new shape P.

b Move shape P down two squares.

Label the new shape Q.

c Describe how to move from shape Q to the original shape.

_____

3.5 Measuring

I can

- use metric measures for length, capacity and mass
- use non-metric measures such as miles

Example

Here are some measurements:　　　**25 mm**　　　**25 cm**　　　**25 m**　　　**25 km**

Which could be the length of

a a running race?　　　　**b** a stamp?　　　　**c** a car park?

Solution

a 25 km　　　*The other three are too short for a race.*

b 25 mm　　　*This is the smallest length in the list.*

c 25 m　　　*An average car is about 4 metres long.*

Practice questions

1　Here are some units of measurement.

grams (g)　　　　　　　kilograms (kg)　　　　　metres (m)

millimetres (mm)　　　　litres (l)　　　　　　　kilometres (km)

Choose the best units to measure these.

a The mass of a bicycle _____

b The length of a pencil _____

c The petrol in a car _____

d The distance between two towns _____

e The mass of a ruler _____

f The height of a building _____

2 Put a sensible metric unit in these sentences.

a My finger is 15 _____ wide.   **b** This room is 5 _____ long.

c My dog weighs 6 _____.   **d** This ruler weighs 15 _____.

3 Measure the length of these lines in millimetres.

a _____   _____ mm

b _____   _____ mm

c _____   _____ mm

4 Write down the lengths, in centimetres, of the lines in Question 3.

a = _____ cm   **b =** _____ cm   **c =** _____ cm

5 The height of a door is 2 metres.

a Write the height in centimetres. _____ cm

b Write the height in millimetres. _____ mm

6 Here is a bottle of spring water.

How many bottles make 1 litre? _____

7 This information is on a website.

From: Liverpool

To: Exeter

Get route

Distance: 253 miles (408 km)
Time: 4 hr 26 min

🖳 Print this page

Say whether each of these statements is true or false. Circle the correct answer.

a A kilometre is shorter than a mile.   True   False

b A mile is less than 2 kilometres.   True   False

8 Milk is sold in pints or in litres.

Here is a milk carton.

Say whether each of these statements is true or false. Circle the correct answer.

a A pint is less than half a litre.   True   False

b Two pints are more than one litre.   True   False

9 Builders always measure lengths in millimetres.

A room is 5 metres long.

Write the length in millimetres. _____ mm

3.6 Time

I can

* use standard units of time

Example

a Write 7:15 pm as a 24-hour clock time.

b How many minutes is it from 7:15 pm to 9:15 pm?

Solution

a 7:15 pm is in the evening.

7 + 12 = 19 so the 24-hour clock time is 19:15.

b 9:15 is two hours after 7:15.

There are 60 minutes in an hour, so two hours is 2 × 60 = 120 minutes.

Practice questions

1 Write down the time on each of these clocks.

a  **b**  **c**

_____   _____   _____

2 Write the 24-hour times for the following. The first one has been done for you.

a 3:00 pm   **15:00**   **b** 9:45 pm   _____

c 10:35 pm   _____   **d** 9:30 am   _____

e 11:52 pm   _____   **f** 2:56 pm   _____

3 Write the 12-hour times for the following.

a 19:00 _____   **b** 14:54 _____

c 16:45 _____   **d** 15:25 _____

e 09:45 _____   **f** 13:56 _____

4 Complete the table.

Time	12-hour clock	24-hour clock
Half past 6 in the morning	6:30 am	06:30
		14:00
	8:30 pm	
10 o'clock in the evening		
		07:15
	2:00 am	
		23:30
Half past midnight		
	3:45 pm	
		02:50

5 Complete the table to convert from hours to minutes.

Hours	1	2	3	4	5	6
Minutes						

Comments, next steps, misconceptions

4 Statistics

4.1 Gathering information

I can
* use a tally chart or record sheet to collect information

Example

This record sheet shows the results of a survey. The survey shows the day of the week some people were born on.

Birthday	Monday	Tuesday	Wednesday	Thursday	Friday	Saturday	Sunday
People	25	31	25	19	25	28	24

a What was the most common day?

b How many were born on a weekend?

Solution

a Tuesday   *This is the day with the highest number of people.*

b 28 + 24 = 52   *Add the numbers for Saturday and Sunday.*

Practice questions

1 Here is a list of the number of brothers and sisters the pupils in a class have.

1   3   1   1   0   3   0   1   0   2   3   1

1   1   1   2   1   0   4   0   2   0   1   2

Collect the information in this table

Number of brothers and sisters	0	1	2	3	4
Number of pupils					

2 The table shows a survey of the type of television programmes a group of Year 12 pupils enjoy most.

Type of programme	Tally	Frequency
Soap operas	卌 卌 卌 卌 卌 III	
Comedy	卌 卌 III	
News	卌 II	
Reality TV	卌 卌 卌	
Drama	卌 卌 I	

Count up the tally marks and fill in the frequency column.

3 a Which is the most popular type of programme? _____

b How many people voted for this? _____

4 a Which is the least popular type of programme? _____

b How many people voted for this? _____

5 How many people enjoy drama programmes the most? _____

6 How many people enjoy comedy programmes the most? _____

7 How many more people chose soap operas than drama as their favourite type of programme? _____

4.2 Statistical diagrams

I can

• construct pictograms and bar charts to record information

Example

This table shows how the people in a company travel to work.

Travel	Car	Bus	Train	Walk
Number	25	45	20	40

Show the results in a pictogram. Use one symbol to represent 10 people.

Solution

You need $2\frac{1}{2}$ symbols for a car, because 25 is $2\frac{1}{2}$ times 10.

Here is a possible answer.

How people travel to work

Car ☐☐◩

Bus ☐☐☐☐◩

Train ☐☐

Walk ☐☐☐

Key ☐ = 10 people

Practice questions

1 This frequency table shows what fruit some pupils ate at lunchtime.

Fruit	Frequency
Apple	8
Orange	12
Banana	14
Nectarine	7

Draw a pictogram to show this data.

Use ☺ to represent two pieces of fruit.

Apple								
Orange								
Banana								
Nectarine								

2 This frequency table shows how many vehicles passed the school gates one morning.

Vehicle	Frequency
Car	60
Van	10
Bicycle	25
Lorry	5

Draw a pictogram using ◇ to represent 10 vehicles.

Car								
Van								
Bicycle								
Lorry								

3 Sally and Tim surveyed their class on eye colour. They recorded their results in the tally chart below.

Eye colour	Tally	Frequency
Blue	‖‖ ‖‖ ‖‖	
Green	‖‖ ‖	
Brown	‖‖ ‖‖ ‖	
Grey	‖	
Other	‖	

a Fill in the frequency column.

b Complete the bar chart.

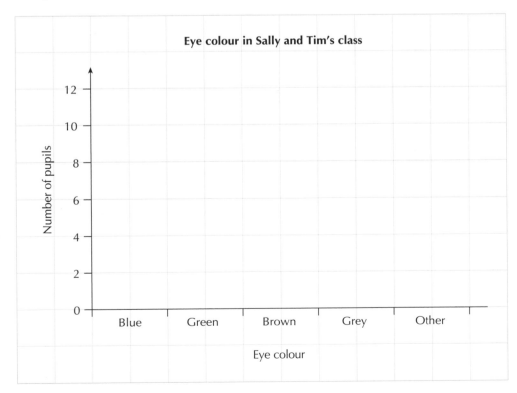

4 Alex asked six of his friends how much television they had watched, in minutes, one evening. The results are shown in the table.

Name	Raj	Juan	Kylie	Gemma	Sunil	Craig
Minutes watched	20	75	30	20	90	45

a Write in the scale for time in the spaces provided on the chart.

Amount of television watched by Alex's friends

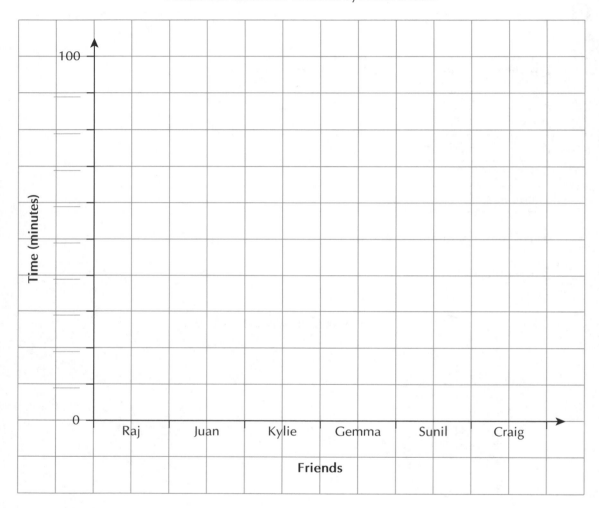

b Complete the bar chart using the data in the table.

c Who watched the most television? _____

d Who watched the least television? _____

4.3 Sorting and classifying information

I can

* use Venn diagrams and Carroll diagrams

Example

This is a Venn diagram.

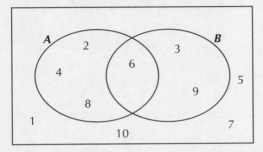

Set A has even numbers.

Set B has numbers in the multiplication table for 3.

Add 11 and 12 to the Venn diagram.

Solution

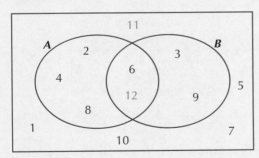

11 is not in either table. It goes outside both sets.

12 is in both tables because it is an even number and it is 4 x 3. It goes in the intersection.

Practice questions

1   **a** Write each number in the correct space in the Carroll diagram.

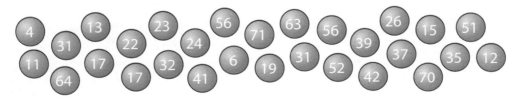

	Red	Blue
Less than 30	◯	◯
More than 30	◯	◯

b Count the numbers in each space on the Carroll diagram. Write the totals in the circle.

c How many numbers are more than 30? _____

d How many blue numbers are less than 30? _____

e How many red numbers are there all together? _____

2 Look at the numbers again.

a Write each number in the correct space on this Carroll diagram.

	Odd	Even
Between 20 and 50	◯	◯
Not between 20 and 50	◯	◯

b Count the numbers in each space on the Carroll diagram. Write the totals in the circle.

c How many odd numbers are there? _____

d How many numbers are between 20 and 50? _____

e How many even numbers are between 20 and 50? _____

f How many odd numbers are **not** between 20 and 50? _____

3 This Venn diagram shows how many pupils play football or hockey.

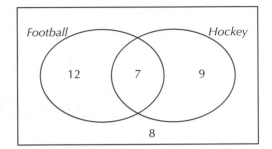

12 pupils play football but not hockey.

a How many play hockey but not football? _____

b How many do not play either sport? _____

c How many play both sports? _____

d How many play football? _____

4.4 Interpreting information

I can

- extract and interpret information in tables, lists, bar charts and pictograms

Example

This bar chart shows the times of cars to drive round a circuit.

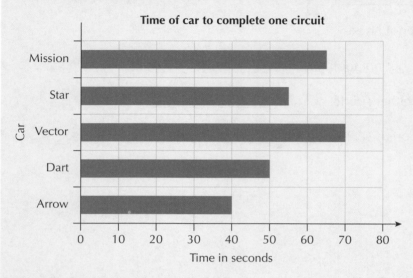

a Which car took the longest time?

b What was the difference between the times of the Arrow and the Star?

Solution

a The Vector   *This is the car with the longest bar.*

b The difference is 55 − 40 = 15 seconds.   *The Arrow took 40 seconds and the Star 55 seconds.*

Practice questions

1 The frequency table shows some flights of planes from a UK airport.

Destination	Frequency
Spain	18
Italy	8
Greece	11
France	6
Portugal	4

a How many planes went to Italy? _____

b What destination had the most planes? _____

c How many more went to Greece than to Portugal? _____

d How many flights are shown all together? _____

2 The chart below shows the distances, in miles, between certain cities in the UK.

Cardiff			
150	London		
398	412	Edinburgh	
246	208	191	York

Complete the sentences.

a The distance from Cardiff to London is _____ miles.

b The distance from London to York is _____ miles.

c The distance from Edinburgh to Cardiff is _____ miles.

d The distance from_____ to _____ is 246 miles.

e The distance from_____ to _____ is 191 miles.

f The distance from_____ to _____ is 412 miles.

3 The bar chart shows the number of days of rain in June in five towns.

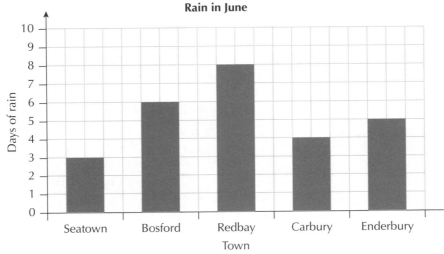

a Write down the number of days of rain in Enderbury. _____

b Which town had most days of rain? _____

c Redbay had more rainy days than Seatown.
How many more? _____

d There are 30 days in June. How many days in
Bosford did not have rain? _____

4. The table shows a bus timetable from Rotherham to Ravenfield.

Rotherham	08:15	09:08
Wickersley	08:38	09:31
Flanderwell	08:42	09:35
Woodlaithes	08:49	09:42
Ravenfield	08:54	09:47

Complete the sentences.

a The buses leave Rotherham at 08:15 and _____

b The 08:15 bus from Rotherham is due at Wickersley at _____

c The 09:08 bus from Rotherham is due at Wickersley at _____

d The 09:08 bus from Rotherham is due at Ravenfield at _____

e From Flanderwell to Woodlaithes it takes_____ minutes.

f From Rotherham to Ravenfield it takes_____ minutes.

5. The table shows the favourite activities of a group of pupils.

	TV	Sport	Computer	Reading
Boys	4	8	6	2
Girls	5	7	3	5

a How many pupils are in the group?

b How many boys chose Sport?

c How many girls chose Computer or Reading?

d How many pupils chose TV?

e Which pastime was the most popular?

f Which pastime was the least popular?

Comments, next steps, misconceptions

Mental warm-up 1: Number

1 Round 4719 to the nearest hundred.
2 $48 \times 9 = 432$. What is $432 \div 9$?
3 Work out $299 + 399$.
4 Work out $35 \div 4$.
5 Tables seat five people. How many tables are needed for 27 people?
6 What is the hundreds digit in 3456?
7 The temperature is 2 °C. It falls by five degrees. What is the new temperature?
8 What fraction of this shape is red? Write your answer as simply as possible.

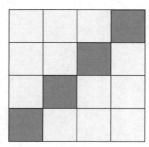

9 Write 83 mm in centimetres.
10 Here is a sequence of numbers:

    30   27   24   21   18

    Write down the next number in the sequence.
11 What units should you use to measure the mass of a pen?
12 How many minutes is $2\frac{1}{2}$ hours?
13 Write 6.45 am in the 24-hour clock.

Mental warm-up 2: Number

1 Round 18.4 to the nearest 10.
2 $13 \times 15 = 195$. What is $195 \div 13$?
3 Work out $97 - 79$.
4 Work out $73 \div 10$.
5 Work out $43 + 69$.
6 Write in figures six hundred and six.
7 What fraction of this shape is red?

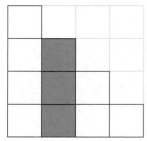

8 The temperature changes from −6°C to −10°C. Has it gone up or down? How many degrees?
9 Write thirty pounds and five pence in figures.
10 Write down the next odd number after 99.
11 A bottle holds 2 litres of water. How many millilitres is that?
12 The time now is 13:45. Write down the time 30 minutes later.

Mental warm-up 3: Geometry and measures

1 Max draws a four-sided shape. All the angles are right angles. It is not a square. What is it?

2 This is a net.

What shape will it make?

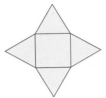

3 All the sides of this shape are the same length.

What is it called?

4 Move triangle A to triangle B.

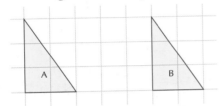

Complete this sentence. It moves _____ squares to the _____.

5 How many faces does a cube have?

6 How many vertices does a square-based pyramid have?

7 Which of the following shapes does **not** have reflection symmetry?

| rectangle | square | parallelogram | kite |

8 Which of these is **not** a net for a cube?

A   B   C

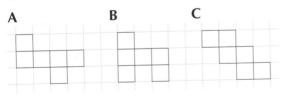

Mental warm-up 4: Statistics

1 This tally chart shows people's age.

Over 65	ЖЖ ‖
21–65	‖‖‖
16–20	ЖЖ ЖЖ ‖
Under 16	‖‖‖

How many people are age 16–20?

2 This pictogram shows the results of a survey of trees.

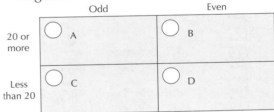

Key = 10 trees

How many trees are elms?

3 Molly is putting numbers in the Carroll diagram.

	Odd	Even
20 or more	A	B
Less than 20	C	D

Should she put the number 30 in cell A, B, C or D?

4 This Venn diagram shows two sets of numbers, A and B.

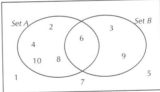

How many numbers are **not** in set B?

5 This pictogram shows where some people went on holiday.

UK	
Europe	
USA	
Asia	
Africa	

15 people stayed in the UK. How many went to Europe?

Collins

Record of achievement certificate

Step 1

Congratulations on achieving Step 1!

Name _____

Date _____

Signed _____